FAMILY ETIQUETTE

WRITTEN BY JAZOE

Table of Contents

Dedications

I wrote this book for my children, and their children, and their children's children...

This book is dedicated to my grandmother, Ina Mae Miles "Mama." Thank you for taking care of us and loving us.

Introduction

I've dealt with lots of secrecy, lies, and many incomplete stories on both sides of my family. My family has either taken their truths to the grave or withheld their most guarded secrets until much later in their adult lives. It's a dysfunctional cycle of not confronting issues head on which often impacts one's love life, how we raise our children, our belief system, and the quality of relationships with other family members which sadly, often remain broken. I want to share with my children all that I know about my family history, their family history; stories about their aunts, uncles, cousins, and grandparents' which will hopefully offer insight into where they come from, which may inform the paths they ultimately forge for their own lives. I want to illustrate for my children, through this narrative, what I have seen with my own eyes and heard through the words of my grandmother, who I lovingly called Mama. I want my children to know the obstacles that we as a family endured and how we triumphantly overcame it all; how love, strength, acceptance, and forgiveness has kept us close to this very day. It is my hope that this book will help to fill in some of the gaps and perhaps help to explain what made me the woman I am today and give some insight about the people who raised me.

PART I

A Broken Family

My father picked us up from Mama's (my grandmother) and we drove down to the Big House in Madera where we stayed with him and his mother, my Granny, until a few days before Christmas. We waived goodbye to Mama before the car left the front of the house. Not one of us were jumping for joy to see him. He bought us plenty of toys, took us to eat pizza and to play pinball. After a few days had passed, my father returned us back to Mama's house in Stockton. I wouldn't see my father until my senior year of high school.

The day after my Mom's birthday and two days before Christmas, two police officers came to Mama's house. As I peered from around the corner of the hallway, I could see the officers at the front door with their big brown hats and badges with the big star emblems. My oldest sister, Jamie, told me to go to the bedroom. I could hear crying coming from the living room shortly before Mama came in to see about me. “What’s wrong Mama?” I asked, looking up at her with worry. “Oh nothin,’ she said. “Your breakfast is ready, com’on and eat.” I followed her down the narrow hallway into the kitchen and sat down. The brightness of the egg yolk-colored walls adorned with a wooden fork and spoon, blinded my eyes as I sat down at the table alongside the rest of my family to eat. Everything Mama made was good, and she would always have a great variety of all the good stuff we kids liked.

Days passed and still my mother had not come to get us. My father had shot my mother when I was five years old leaving me and my siblings to be raised by my grandmother while my mother clung to life, recovering in the hospital ICU. Our separation from my mother, and our time with my grandmother, made my siblings and I even tighter. Unbeknownst to me, I wouldn’t see my mother again for several weeks.

My parents were both raised on the southside of Stockton, California, and attended Edison High School. My dad, James, was a sports jock who excelled in football, track, and basketball. He was strikingly handsome with smooth, dark chocolate skin without a blemish to be found. He was also highly intelligent. My mother, Alice, was and still is stunningly beautiful, with a sweet, kind spirit that attracts everyone who meets her. Mom became pregnant with my oldest sister, Jamie, during her senior year of high school, which changed both of my parents lives forever.

While my father was brilliant, athletically gifted, musically talented and loved by so many people, he was a horrible husband and father. He used drugs and alcohol regularly and was very abusive to my mother, my sisters Jamie and Jai, and my brother James. It didn't seem to matter to him that he had a great family and a loving wife. It seemed more of a chore being with his family and he proved incapable of expressing his love at home. He wanted the picturesque image of the perfect family, without the burden and responsibility. My mother always credited him with being an excellent provider though. We lived in the best homes, and *he* drove the best cars.

However, my mother was left with an old beater for us to push around town in. The centerpiece of our living room was his piano, while we spent most of our time in the game room upstairs or playing in our big backyard. While each week, he dutifully turned over his weekly paycheck to my mother, my father was mostly absent from our daily lives. On the occasions when he was present, he was unpredictable and very abusive.

From the day they hooked up, my father cheated on my mother with countless women of different races and backgrounds and the infidelity never ceased. Around 1967, with three small children at home, he left Stockton to attend Utah State University on an athletic scholarship. There he began dating a foreign student whose family was of high social stature in her home country. One day my mother received a phone call from the girl, confessing her love for my dad. She said that they had been seeing each other for quite some time, and that she wanted him to return to her country with her, but he had refused. I never understood why my mother remained with him when he showed her no love, respect, or compassion. She said she thought that she could change him. She had witnessed her own mother's abuse at her father's hand most of her life and learned an unwavering tolerance. At times she would confront him about his cheating, but he always denied it.

After completing college my father had the choice of either playing professional basketball or football. He chose the latter. He packed up the family and moved to Denver where he started training camp with the Denver Broncos. During the off-season, he would play semi-professional basketball. As he always had, my dad would turn over his paycheck to my mom and she would place the checks under the mattress because she had never had or seen that much money in her life.

Despite the good money and comfortable lifestyle, the entire family was miserable, including my father. My mother and my siblings missed my grandmother and the rest of our family in California. While playing football in Denver, my father became injured and the family returned to California. Shortly after our return, my father left for a quick stint playing for the Canadian Football League, leaving my mother and my siblings behind. A few months later, he returned home for good.

My mother did clerical work for the Port of Stockton, as she had since she graduated from high school. Lucky for her, when she returned from Denver, she was able to get her old job back. My father secured a job working for PG&E making great money, but he hated it. My father also still played travel basketball while continuing to gamble and abuse drugs and alcohol. On October 8, 1972, my mother went into labor while my dad was glued to the Cincinnati Bengals/Denver Broncos game. Despite the pain of contractions, he told my mother to wait until the next touchdown before he would take her to the hospital to deliver me. The Bengals beat the Broncos 21 to 10.

My experience with my father was quite different from that of my sisters and my brother. Although he was a towering figure at six foot-three inches tall and about two hundred-fifteen pounds, there is little that I remember about my father's presence in my childhood. I fondly recall how I would ride his back, dance on top of his feet, and hug his neck. Despite him never initiating hugs or playful moments with me, he also never rejected me. "You made him play with you," my mother recalled. He called me "The Baby." For my siblings, growing up in the 70's, in a white, Brady Bunch-like neighborhood wasn't easy. There were many instances when they had to defend themselves and one another. Jamie, James, and Jai very tight, the result of being stair step kids born closely one after the other.

Sports has always played a role in my life in one way or another. There was no escaping it. My father was inducted into the Stockton Black Sports Hall of Fame for track, basketball, and football. My mom was a premier softball player and participated in the Women's World Series for Softball in Toledo, Ohio. She began playing softball in the sixth grade as a means of escape from life at home with her abusive father, and later in adulthood as temporary retreats from my abusive father. Mom played softball the entire nine months she carried me in her belly and for years after I was born. For the first six seasons of my life, I grew up at the softball complex at Louis Park in west Stockton, where my mom's teammates, The Rancher's Raiders, became our extended family. This group of young women hailed from a variety of backgrounds. Their coach, Bob, a member of the Hells Angels motorcycle club always caught hell for coaching a team of mostly "niggas and spicks." But Bob didn't care. The Rancher's Raiders became the all-time greats of their time. As the oldest player on the team and with four kids in tow, my mom was given the nickname "Momma" by her teammates. Scorching, hot days at Louis Park were where we wanted to be. We traveled all over California with the team. Those were some of the happiest times of our lives, filled with memories we continue to hold dear. That was our escape.

My grandmother, who we called Mama, was also our escape. She cleaned the homes of fancy white folks close to where we lived. Often after work, Mama would come by and sometimes spend the night. My sister Jai and Mama were very close, and she often served as my family's temporary shield from our fathers' abuse. He was never mean or abusive when others were around, but when they left, his reign of terror resumed. Instilling fear in his family guaranteed that they would stay in their place. He would proclaim that he was the "King," and our family were to do as he commanded.

My mother would often hear her children crying from behind the closed door of their bedroom, but she dare not open it for fear of being beaten herself or securing a more severe beating for her kids. He would say that he was whooping my brother and sisters so that they would be good. He would ask each of them how many licks they wanted "twenty-five or fifty?" My siblings were given the option to take swats for each other, which they did often. My father's terrorism continued for years until the fall of 1977 when my mother had mustered up the courage to devise a plan to leave my father.

We had recently moved into a beautiful home in a predominantly white neighborhood in the Lincoln District of North Stockton. In the 1970's that was a big deal, as Black folks rarely crossed the north side of Park Street. My father was well known and respected in both the streets and with important white folks in town. He had many close friends and associates in high and low places that he had known for years. Some would come over for dinner parties and evening socials, but my mom never spoke a word about of our life at home or the abuse we endured, not even to family. I'm certain that her co-workers and some family members knew about the abuse, but during that time people didn't speak out about domestic violence, and victims didn't seek out help, counseling or resources for themselves and their children.

The night before my father had beaten my mom pretty bad and vowed that after she got home from work that he would finish what he had started. She knew that she had to escape before he killed her. Throughout the day, he would call her at work taunting her of with what was to come. Terrified, she called my oldest sister Jamie, who was home from school that day. She told her to pack our clothes and to keep an eye out for our cousin Regina who would take her to pick up the rest of the kids from school and drop us off at Mama's house. When my mother arrived at Mama's, we piled into my uncle's car, and he drove us from Stockton to my Ant-T's house in Oakland. My mother was terrified, replaying in her mind my dad's promise that he would kill her if she ever tried to leave. Before that day she had never left, opting instead to live a lie to protect herself and her children. To some of the world our family appeared perfect, but mom was hallowed and empty inside. I can't remember much of what happened when I was six years old, but I remember that drive, somber and quiet. Despite the heaviness of that moment, my mom engaged us all in small talk and did her best to make us smile, always making things seem not as bad as they truly were. Not until I was twelve years old, did I understand that the look in her eyes, the look in my siblings' eyes that I had never seen before, it was fear of the consequence of us running away.

We were blessed to have my Ant-T, my mom's oldest sister, who took in my mother and her four children with no hesitation. She had three of her own children at home who were a little older than my sisters and my brother. So, there we were, all nine of us living in a two-bedroom apartment on Davis Avenue in Oakland, where we would remain until my mom could get back on her feet.

Once he realized we were really gone, the reality that the seemingly perfect world he had constructed was crumbling around him. He had really done it this time. My father didn't write checks, iron clothes, cut hair, or cook his own dinner. My mother had done all that. Whispers spread among family members and friends that his drug use was getting worse. He searched everywhere for us. Eventually he got wind that we were in Oakland and before long, he had tracked us down. One day at my school, my mom saw him watching her as she dropped me off. She quickly ran back into the school and informed the office staff that her husband, who had threatened to kill her, had followed her to the school. By the time the police arrived, he was long gone. Heart pounding through her chest, she jumped into her car and punched it through the streets of Oakland, her car flying through mid-air, and leaping over hills in her pursuit of my aunt's apartment. When she arrived, she darted from the car into the apartment, the car engine still running, where she stayed for days, afraid to leave.

Three months passed since we had fled and after many failed attempts to reach us, my mother's attorney made arrangements for my dad to see us during the Christmas holiday. We would all be going to Granny's in Madera. It didn't really matter to me when I found out we were going to see him, and I hadn't spent a lot of time with Granny like I had with Mama. I loved my Granny though and she was something else. She never missed one day of work at the cannery in fifty years. She loved fishing, dipping snuff, and she was known to keep a razor in her bosom and a piece in her glove box. She wasn't much of a hugger, but Granny loved all her family. My grandfather Elliot had passed away when my father was a teen, and Granny never remarried. She didn't really meddle in my parent's affairs, but she would tell my mother, "as long as he is bringing you the check, it doesn't matter what he doing."

I vaguely remember getting in the big clean car my dad was driving when he came to pick us up from Mama's house for the long ride to Madera. Neither my sister Jai nor my brother James wanted to go in the first place. My brother who my father called Pap just wanted peace, and Jai who my father called Pig just couldn't stand him. She had asked my mother on several occasions, "why don't you just leave him." She was the only one of his kids to dare challenge his authority. Jai recalls, "He was whooping James with a radiator belt, and I grabbed the belt from him and yelled, I hate you, I hate you!!" He dropped the belt and walked away sobbing. That was the only time he had ever listened to any of them.

However, it was too late to get out of that trip. The arrangements had been made and we were headed to Granny's. While we were in Madera, my mother continued to work each day, trying to adjust to her new life without having to look over her shoulder. My mom's cousin Cookie, with whom she is still close, got her a job working as a warehouse packer in Emeryville, a few miles from my aunt's apartment in Oakland. My cousin would pick her up from work at night.

After returning to Stockton from Madera, my father dropped off my siblings and I at Mama's house. I didn't know it then, but that would be the last time I would see him until I was a senior in high school. He quickly set out to locate my mother and see through the threats he had made. Having dropped us off in Stockton, he was assured that we weren't with her. He knew where to find her. He changed into his brown PG&E uniform and drove his work truck to Oakland. He simply needed to wait until she returned home from work.

Once he arrived, my father staked out my Ant-T's apartment, blending into the neighborhood by pretending to work on a PG&E project in that area. When my mother arrived home from work that night, my father, hidden under the staircase near the front door of Ant-T's apartment, crept out from the shadow underneath the staircase with a sawed off shot gun and opened fire on my mother. "James, no," she screamed! Two shots blazed from the barrel, the first was a miss, and the second nearly blew off her arm. My cousin saw my father flee the bloodied scene. He kicked open the front door of the apartment, pulled my mother in to safety, and they called 911. My mother dragged herself across the living room floor and into my Ant' T's bedroom where she collapsed. Feathers from the pillow she used to shield her arm from the gun fire, which ultimately saved her life, were scattered everywhere. She had debated whether to bring the pillow with her to work that day to sit on because for the first time in her life she had a hemorrhoid flare up, and at work she would often be sitting down. My Ant' T warned, "okay, you leave that pillow at work and you won't have one to sleep on." Ultimately, she decided to take the pillow and that decision had saved her life.

As they waited impatiently for the ambulance to arrive, my aunt frantically wrapped my mom's arm in a cake box that they had planned to use for a holiday cake they were baking that night. The cake box provided her arm the support to keep it attached and in place until the ambulance arrived. By the time the ambulance arrived a crowd had gathered outside the apartment complex. From the crowd my father watched as they rushed my mom from the apartment, en route to Highland General Hospital, as my father trailed behind the ambulance. As she drifted in and out of consciousness, my mother said she heard my aunt screaming, "Bitch, don't chu' die on me!"

When she arrived at the hospital my mother's body was covered in blood which masked the wound and making it difficult to determine from where she was bleeding. The anesthesiologist explained her apprehension in sedating my mom and that putting her under may result in her not waking up. "Do what you have to do," she told the doctor, "I just don't wanna die." She began to recite the Lord's Prayer, "Our Father, which art in Heaven..." All night long, while they poked, prodded, cut, and inserted tubes into her body with no anesthesia to dull the pain, she continued to pray. "For thine is the kingdom, and the power and the glory, forever." Miraculously, she survived.

My father shot my mother on her thirty-first birthday. Witnesses recounted seeing my father walking around the hospital but reported that he left the scene before the police were able to apprehend him. Upon attaining a detailed description, the police hunted him until he was found a few days later at his girlfriend's apartment in Stockton.

In the aftermath of my mother's shooting, my grandmother was right there with us through it all, making us feel loved and as comfortable as she could. Each night I slept with Mama. Over and over again, I would ask “where is my momma and when is she coming to get me?” After a few weeks had passed, my Aunty Brenda, who also lived with my grandmother, drove us to Highland Hospital in Oakland to see our mother. With her arm held up by a sling, she lay in a hospital bed on the eighth floor. The same floor as jail inmates, so she that she had 24-hour security. I remember looking out of the window in her room where I could see the parking lot, still confused about what had happened to her. “When are you coming to get me” I asked? “Soon,” she replied. “Be good and listen to Mama.”

PART II

We Had Mama

Domestic violence was largely ignored in the legal and social realms of 1970's California with virtually no laws existing to protect battered women. Granny hired the best lawyers to defend my father and by the time it was all over he was sentenced to only three years in prison for aggravated assault. He served a year and a half, with a legal floater imposed which prevented him from returning to Stockton. His sentence was far less than most felt he deserved.

While my mother lay in a hospital bed recovering from the gunshot wound that nearly ended her life, my father, the man who shot her, had been arrested and confined to a jail cell. Neither of our parents were able to care for us, but we had our maternal grandmother, Mama. My father's family has always been and still is, as loving, supportive, and available as my mom's family, and despite the horrendous actions of my father, his family never allowed our relationship to fade. From time to time, we would receive clothes and birthday cards with cash from my father's family. My mother's lifelong friend Ingrid with whom she is still best friends to this day, always looked out for us and my grandmother. She would visit and bring food, clothes, and anything else she thought we needed.

I recall my dad's mother, my granny, picked me up once and took me with her to Madera for a few days when she had time off work from the cannery. The drive to Madera was long and Granny wasn't much of a talker. There weren't any cell phones or hand-held devices at that time to keep me entertained until we reached our destination. Before we hit the Highway 99, she would buy me a burger, fries, and something to drink from Sno-White Drive-In on Mariposa Road. By the time I finished eating my food and listening to Granny on her CB Radio for a while, I was out like a light for the rest of our two-hour trip to Madera.

When we arrived in Madera there was plenty of family there. My great-great grandmother, who we called Little Granny would be there, helping at the family's care home which was just down the street from the big house. Little Granny lived to be over hundred years old, and her eyes were a beautiful grayish blue. Granny's sister, my Aunt Odessa who was also her best friend, ran the care home and owned other businesses. She also had property in Stockton. Both Granny and Aunt OD often traveled to Stockton to check on things, and they both loved to dress. Aunt OD was the best. She was fearless. A pretty lady, with big hips and plenty of sass. I miss her.

Granny stayed busy, and from the time she got to Madera until she left, her days were filled with work and cooking. We would walk up and down the street all day and then spend time working in the backyard. At night after I took my bath, I would crawl into her bed and sleep with Granny just as I slept with Mama in Stockton, but it wasn't the same. I missed Mama, and after a few days in Madera, Granny would drive me back to Stockton and drop me back off to her. I couldn't wait to see Mama, but I always appreciated Granny and the time I spent with her.

At six years old, my mother was gone, and Mama became my world. At that time, there was no place I would rather be than with my siblings and my grandmother. We had a nice home in a new housing development on the southside of Stockton known as Sharpe's Lane. We had clothes on our backs, shoes on our feet, love, family, and good food. My mother tells me now, "Mama didn't like to cook like ya'll think she did. But she had too, with seven kids and then ya'll." No one could've told me that, as she moved around that kitchen effortlessly, like Top Chef before Top Chef. She was so in her element, in her natural environment, and seemed at peace doing it. My siblings and I enjoyed the privilege and blessing daily, of watching her create delicious comfort foods and savory dishes.

Although sifters, measuring cups and spoons filled the drawers of her kitchen, rarely did I see her measure ingredients. She opted for the convenience of a coffee cup from the cabinet shelf to measure a cup of flour, sugar, milk, or any other ingredient, adding a dash of this and a pinch of that to flavor a dish. She did most of her baking on Sundays and holidays, but she always kept cookies in the cookie jar. And who didn't love her fried pies with apple or peach filling? "Mama would cut up the peaches and use burlap and paper bags to dry them on top of the roof of the house when we were kids," my mom remembers. Her candied yams drenched in a thick, buttery, bubbling brown sugar bath that coated them like candy. Mama's fried fish with smothered potatoes is still a family favorite we all cook to this day. My oldest sister, Jamie, loved her fried chicken, skillet corn, with rice and gravy. Seasoned salt, garlic powder and Mrs. Dash didn't occupy space on Mama's pantry shelf. She only used salt and pepper to flavor the chicken and it was perfectly seasoned to the bone. Her cast iron skillets were seasoned and fried her chicken to perfection. A coffee can with a strainer on top, sat next to the stove to collect grease for the next fry. She could mix two different flavors of Kool-Aid that tasted better than any soda.

My mother's two oldest brothers didn't live with us at Mama's, but they would visit from time to time. Her two younger brothers and her youngest sister did however, live at home, although their busy schedules kept them away from the house a lot. My Aunty Brenda attended University of the Pacific where she pursued her Bachelor of Arts in Special Education. The youngest of the uncles spent his days riding his motorcycle anywhere the road would take him, while my other Uncle worked as a truck driver and a mechanic.

As the youngest of my mother's four children, eight years younger than my oldest sister and six years younger than the next youngest, I could never go anywhere with them. Every blue moon they would allow me to tag along, but not very often. Occasionally my sister Jamie would take me with her to the mall or to visit one of her friends who had kids at their house my age who I could play with. My sister Jai would take me to her basketball games, softball games, or to the park to play on the swings while she played basketball. It was my brother, however, who spent the most time with me. Although he had friends and cousins his age that he could hang out with, he was mostly a loner. Though seven years older than me, he would still take the time to show me how to fly a kite or ride a bike and burn things with a magnifying glass. There were times, however, when he too would leave me behind which was too much for my soul to bare.

The highlight of my time at Mama's house was time spent with my little cousin. Who was my mother's youngest brother's daughter. We were only two years apart and raised more like sisters. My life was so much better when she was there. We fought, and I wasn't always the best cousin or role model, but we had each other. She needed me just as much as I needed her. Both of our lives, though different, were very similar. She would spend the weekends with us and go back to her other grandmother's house during the week. We would cry to be with one another and then fight once we were together again.

Some days were harder than others without my mom, especially when my cousin had gone home, and I was left alone. But Mama always found a way to make those days brighter. We would listen to music while I watched her cook. She would share with me stories about her life growing up as a young girl in Gilmer, Texas and about her husband, my grandpa Cha'ly. Mama's stories were the best and as I got older the stories became even more intriguing. I would ask her questions for hours and hours until she was tired.

She once told me that in her day, when people died, "they didn't take 'um to a funeral home." The body would remain in the house for a few days which was the equivalent of today's wake. The body was placed on what they called a cooling board; a perforated wooden platform on which the body would be temporarily stored and prepared for the funeral. Ice was placed underneath to keep the body chilled, slowing the decomposition process. She said, “People would be lined up down the street, bringing potato salad and fried chicken.” Mama’s family was big in the church and had a cemetery named after them filled with her relatives and neighbors, in Gilmer where it remains today. “Wow,” I thought, “she’d seen a lot of dead folks by the time she was my age.” Eyes wide-with amazement, I sat at the table and listened attentively as she cooked and shared her stories.

Mama was born in in 1917. Like most young girls, she adored her father who she called, Poppa. “He was a cattle herder,” she would say proudly. “The white folks would pay him to herd their cattle from one place to another.” Her mother, my great grandma was a Christian homemaker. Mama’s aunt was a schoolteacher. The family owned a general store, and their house sat on acres of land owned by her father. This was a huge accomplishment for a Black family in the 1920’s rural south and she was proud to share it. She never claimed her family to be rich, but they weren’t poor. Mama’s mother was strict, and she didn’t play when it came to attending church each day, which left Mama very little time to do anything else. Attending church was non-negotiable. "Church, church, church, we all had to go to church," she'd say.

Mama's husband Charles, who everyone called Cha'ly, was also from Gilmer, though he experienced a quite different up bringing than Mama. He was the total opposite of her in every way. Unlike Mama's family, his family had little money. His father was said to be a preacher who drank and ran around town with different women and had a few different families. Cha'ly didn't care much care for him and decided to carry his mother's last name. "Why did you run off with him?" I asked Mama. "Momma was so tight on me," she responded. "So, the minute I got a taste of life, I jumped at it. I left with Cha'ly during the Heaven or Hell Dance at the Church, and it's been hell every-since." She said, Cha'ly didn't mind no rules, and he cussed and fought all the time.

Mama's first two children were born on an old farm where Mama and Cha'ly lived during the 1930s. They were provided lodging and pay. Mama knew that after she had left home that going back was not an option. She'd made her bed, and now she would have to lie in it. So, they made their own way by selling moonshine and him working odd jobs. Until the opportunity for Cha'ly to work on the railroad came. He would leave from Gilmer for work, then send for his family soon after to meet him in California.

Mama told me that she heard stories about California; fruit trees everywhere, sandy beaches and a better life than the one she knew in Texas. She heard that you could just pick fruit right off the trees that bordered the highway. Ant'T recalled the day she, Mama, and my Uncle Jimmy boarded the train headed to California. She told me that her grandfather dropped them off. That they had a shoebox lunch, with fried chicken and cake for their long ride to California. Uncle Jimmy vaguely recalls having lived in Los Angeles when he was about five years old. The family lived in a hotel for Black people with a communal kitchen and bathroom facilities, owned by a

Black woman. Ant'T recalled when she replied, "yes, ma'am," to one of the ladies in hotel. She told her that she was no longer in Texas and that in California she didn't have answer no ma'am. Yes, no, and thank you was quite enough. The hotel sat on a busy downtown street where streetcars passed all throughout the day, reminiscent of a set from the film "Devil in a Blue Dress."

Ant'T and Uncle Jimmy recall, the day Uncle Jimmy was crossing the street in Los Angles as they were on their way to the picture show. A strong wind blew his hat off his head. Reflexively, he darted into the street to retrieve his hat without noticing the oncoming streetcar. Ant'T snatched him back before the streetcar hit him.

Mama, Cha'ly and their kids had been in Los Angeles only a few months before Mama's baby brother, Buford, who she was close to, came to stay with them for a spell. Unc had fled Gilmer after a dice game had gone bad with some white boys, where one of the boys cheated and Unc busted him in his head. Fearing for his life, his family put him on a train and sent him to Los Angeles. He wasted no time adjusting to life in California. He quickly discovered the most happening spots in town and got a job working at a shipyard. He told the story about how he got a hold of an etiquette book which changed his life forever. He was able to learn the game of etiquette. Which allowed him access to be in places he would have never imagined being in, and he was taking it all in. Sometime later, he enlisted in the service and fought in the Korean War. When he returned from the war, he became a tailor by trade and a businessman by pure wit. Unc would continue to visit often throughout the years. Both Mama and their sister, my Aunt Susie who lived in Fresno with her family.

By 1946, Mama and Cha'ly had relocated to the southside of Stockton in an area known as Sharpe's Lane. Cha'ly worked at the railroad yard and Mama took care of their small shack and the children. Just before Christmas, Mama gave birth to her fourth child, my mother Alice, the first of Mama's children born in California. Mama would have three more children, bringing her total to seven.

One winter, my mother became extremely sick, so ill that her lips turned blue, but Cha'ly wouldn't allow Mama to take her to the hospital. Unc, had returned home from the war and popped in to visit. He took one look at my mother and rushed her to the hospital where she was diagnosed with pneumonia. Unc saved my mother's life, and they would forever share a special bond.

Neither my mother, nor her siblings, ever hid from us how poor they had been and how they had lived in a dilapidated shack while growing up. At night from their beds, they could see the stars through the holes in their roof. How they had an outhouse for restroom. Ant'T recalled the day Mama went into labor with my mother. "It was pouring raining," she said, and they were living in a trailer that was parked in a dirt lot that had turned to mud from all the rain. During this era of a mass migration from the south to California. Many blacks moved from the Southern States to California to escape not only the oppression, but for better jobs and a better life for their families. When new families arrived they just had the land, so the neighborhood would help with building the home. From the foundation to the construction, but Cha'ly didn't want that. His family first lived in a tent on their lot of dirt land, then a trailer, then a shack. The truth is, they didn't have to live like that. But Cha'ly would have it no other way. He refused to spend his hard-earned money on his family. "He'd drink it up with his friends," Mama said. Leaving her to hustle food, blankets, clothes and whatever else they needed to survive. As neglectful as he was, leaving Cha'ly and returning to Gilmer was still not an option. Mama had been raised comfortably with all her needs having been met which was quite different from what Cha'ly had experienced. She believed that Cha'ly did what he did to bring her down a peg. Yet Mama still maintained her pride and her dignity through it all. She wasn't tall, just about five two, very pretty and "high yella" as they called it in those days; always clean and nicely dressed.

As Cha'ly's drinking and abuse continued, the older children would assume additional responsibilities for helping Mama care for their younger siblings, as best they could. Ant' T, my mother's oldest sister attended school to become a nurse and eventually moved out of the house into her own place not too far from Mama. She continued to help Mama and take care of her own family that she now had. Ant'T eventually moved to Oakland where she would raise her children, but still continued to help. Ant'T gave my mother the best Christmas ever my mom recalls, "I had so many toys and a beautiful doll." But when the flood came not too long after. My Mom had to leave all her toys. Uncle Jimmy saw no way out if he stayed in Stockton, and after getting into it with Cha'ly again about Mama he left home for the military, a day my mother remembers as one of the saddest days for her. She said that she cried and cried, but she knew he had to go. Uncle Jimmy was leaving to become a better man than his father and wanted to help Mama. He would leave on a bus headed to San Francisco where he would then be stationed out. But, when he arrived to check in, he was malnourished and didn't pass the weight requirement to be recruited. Uncle Jimmy pleaded with the Sergeant that he couldn't go back home to his father. The Sergeant understood and worked out arrangements with a local hotel. So, for two weeks he was to eat, rest and get prepared to be stationed out. Which he did, and was sent to Fort Ord in Marina, California. With Uncle Jimmy gone, the younger brothers who were able to work, did and provided. Finally, in 1964, Mama left Cha'ly for good. He would eventually show up in front of the house cutting up and acting a fool, but Mama's now much older sons warned that he didn't want think about taking it there. In less than a decade later, in 1971 and a year before I was born, Cha'ly died.

As time passed, Mama began working more outside of the house. Sometime in the early 1970's she got a job working as a seamstress and presser for an upscale boutique called the House of Nine's on the Miracle Mile in Stockton. The boutique only sold clothes in a size nine. The Miracle Mile was a predominately white area in those days. The only Blacks one would see were those working in the stores. Often, because she was Black, she encountered racist situations. But Mama had pride and standards for herself, and she refused to be taken advantage of simply because she needed a job. Eventually, she quit House of Nine's because as she said, "I was there to work and not to kiss nobody's ass."

Mama continued to work in the same well to do area though, but now as a housekeeper. The homes in that area which were north of Park Street and not too far from the University of the Pacific, were gorgeous and some were even mansions. She eventually became both a nanny and housekeeper for a woman named Barbara Fass, who would later become Stockton's first female mayor. She was an amazing woman and the daughter of German-Jewish immigrants. She worked very closely with minority communities and collaborated with Cesar Chavez to confront problems facing farm laborers. She also worked on issues of equality and desegregation. She called Mama, "Mama" just as we did. Many years later, Barbara represented my mother in court when she divorced my father. She and my mom remained good friends for many years until they eventually lost touch. Sadly, Barbara passed away in 2020 at the age of 80 years old. She left an amazing legacy, and our family will never forget her or her kind, loving heart.

Needless to say, my mother's childhood wasn't ideal and as she lay in her hospital bed recovering from her gunshot wounds, she reflected on it all. Days, weeks, and months would pass before she would finally be discharged from the hospital but not before she had to endure a seemingly endless series of weekly surgeries to restore minimal functionality of her left arm. Each time she was wheeled from her room to the operating room, she was filled with terror, certain that my father was still out there waiting, ready to finish the job. She lived in constant fear that she wouldn't wake up from the surgery, fearful that she would die on the operating table.

One morning, a stranger, Ms. Jeff, came to my mother's room to take her to surgery. My mother was curious as to why George, the surgical technician that she had grown comfortable with, and who had become the calming force she was accustomed to seeing before her next operation, wasn't there. George was kind and made her feel safe. Apprehensive, she expressed her concern of going with Ms. Jeff, fearful that she would die. Anxiously she asked, "where's George?" Ms. Jeff told her that George wasn't in today and that "God sent me to give you a message." She told my mom that she had nothing to be afraid of and that if it had been meant for her to die, she would have died when the man whom she had worshipped like a god for so long, had shot her.

"I heard about you," she continued. "They've been talking all over this hospital about you; about the woman who should have been dead." She told my mother that she had known of her before the ambulance brought her to the hospital. She explained that my Ant' T, with whom Ms. Jeff worked at the hospital with, had shared her sister's story of running from her abusive husband. "They say you prayed all night while they worked on you with no anesthesia, so know that God saved you for a purpose, so that you can be a living testimony," Ms. Jeff reminded her. Referring to the night that my mother was brought in and had refused anesthesia terrified that if she were put under, she would never wake up. She continued to calm and reassure my mother that she had nothing to fear and that she would be just fine. They prayed as she wheeled her to and from surgery. She and Ms. Jeff became close friends, and as the months passed my mother got better and stronger. Then one morning I woke up to mother's beautiful face. I was certain that I was dreaming. A cast encased her damaged arm, but she was there, back at Mama's house. She had finally come to get us. A few months passed before we were able to leave with her as she had to secure a place for us to live.

PART III

I Hella Love Oakland

I grew up between two cities an hour apart, Stockton and Oakland. The summer after the shooting, I went to Oakland to spend the summer with my mother at my Ant' T's new apartment. My cousins all still lived with my aunt, and one of my cousins had just given birth to her baby boy. While my mother and my aunt worked during the day, I would spend time with my cousin and her baby. I adored her baby and he adored me. I would carry him on my hip all throughout the house acting as if he were my baby. Though older, my cousins were so patient, kind, and loving. They understood what we had gone through because they had gone through it with us. I remember one of my cousins was a DJ. He had an amazing vinyl collection. It was the first time I remember seeing an album cover. It was Heatwave with the melting record, and Parliament with the spaceship. My other cousin liked to dance. I would watch Soul Train with her. It was a great summer, but I wasn't ready to move yet to Oakland yet.

Neither me nor my sisters were ready to leave Stockton. They both were into school and sports, and I knew that I would miss Mama. So, Mama and my mother agreed that we could stay in Stockton for a little while longer. We would visit Oakland throughout the year as it was only an hour drive, and my mother would call us all the time. We knew we could move there whenever we wanted, but we weren't yet ready, and my mom wasn't quite settled. However, when my brother James got into trouble for cutting class in Stockton, my mom made us all move to Oakland. James was the only one of us truly ready to leave Stockton.

We missed Stockton and Mama, and eventually my mother and Mama gave in and allowed us girls to move back to Stockton until my oldest sister Jamie, a high school junior, graduated. My brother remained in Oakland with my mother, and it would be just the two of them for about a year and a half. When it came time for us to move again to Oakland, my middle sister Jai stayed in Stockton to finish school and continued playing basketball. She was now a junior in high school and had received recruitment offers to attend UOP, San Jose State, and a few other colleges. Ultimately, she accepted a four-year basketball scholarship to San Jose State, which was ideal because she would only be about thirty minutes from us in Oakland. We were all proud and happy for her. It was a tough time for me with so much for me to process. I was young and torn between Mama and my mother, but my mother made it clear that I was leaving Mama's and moving to Oakland.

Around 1981, a disabled gentleman hired my mother as a cashier in the gift shop at Highland General Hospital, the same hospital she had been brought to, almost dead from a gunshot wound. The owner soon became ill and was no longer able to run the business, so he gifted the gift shop to my mother. She was now a business owner, but we still had very little money. She declined all child and spousal support from my father, choosing to be the sole source of support for all of us.

Upon turning eighteen, my oldest sister Jamie got a job working for the City of Oakland to help my mother take care of the family. We moved around a few times and even stayed at a motel in a nice area in Alameda. It was during this time and for the first time, that I attended a predominately white school. Only me and three other Black kids attended that school. Some of the white kids were nice but others were downright mean. I, however, never had a problem standing up for myself.

We lived in Alameda for about a year before my mom moved us into a house in East Oakland. However, I had to finish the remainder of the school year at the school in Alameda. My fifth-grade teacher, Mr. Delacruz, though Filipino, was just as bad as the white teachers. Mr. Delacruz ignored the many openly racist remarks hurled at me from the white students. One day Mr. Delacruz announced that we would stage a production of Grease to be performed at the school program, and he began assigning roles. I asked to play Sandy, the female lead of the musical. A girl in my class blurted out, “You can’t be Sandy, you’re Black!” Mr. Delacruz told her to please be quiet and continued to pass out parts. He did not address the inappropriate statement with the student. I was angrier than hurt. I didn’t get a part but was assigned to the chorus of students not chosen for main roles, to participate in the dance numbers. That is my first recollection of having dealt with racism, and by the end of the day my brain was exhausted from having tried to make sense out of it.

I didn’t have conversations with my mother about my experiences with racism at school. She was always busy working at either the gift shop or at her other job at the City of Oakland. Most of our time together was at night when she would cook, talk a little, eat, love on us, pray, sleep, and prepare to do it all again the next day. Most weekends I worked with her at the gift shop where I would run the cash register. That was a big job at my age, and I was the boss for the day. She'd teach me how to make floral arrangements and take inventory. I'd roll pennies and organize receipts. On the weekdays when I got out of school, I would either ride the bus to the gift shop in Oakland to meet her, or I would walk approximately two miles to our house. My mother had no idea I was making that trek alone, but my brother had showed me this route.

Sometimes he walked with me, but other times I was alone because he either had practice or he was just hanging with his friends. However, I was never afraid. There was something special about that walk from my elementary school in Alameda to our house in East Oakland. I only had to cross the High Street Bridge and I was back in Oakland. As I walked through the beautiful tree lined blocks of immaculate homes and yards, I would contemplate the life I wanted to live when I grew up. I never saw other Black people until I crossed the bridge into Oakland, and when I did, I was in a whole new world. Stinky factories, the Clorox company, metal shops, and a row of blocks upon blocks of industrial area. Alameda and Oakland were night and day. Along my journey home, I would sing the songs of my favorite artists. It took about forty-five minutes to get home, but the time would fly by. Even though we lived in the hood and struggled sometimes, I never felt like we were broke. I had everything I thought I needed.

My brother James was a senior at Alameda High School, not far from my school, where he played sports. He was very popular for the short time he was there and happy to be at a new school where no one knew about our family tragedy. James was both an honor roll student and a star athlete, excited about the prospect of attending college on a sports scholarship. One fall Friday night, Alameda played against a team from Stockton, our family's hometown. The Stockton coach immediately recognized my brother's name as being the same as a star athlete he had known, my father. Having heard the story of my dad, a local celebrity, who had shot his wife, he relayed the gossip to my brother's Alameda coach. My brother's coach, in turn, confided in someone else details of the incident and before long, the gossip had spread like wildfire throughout the entire school. James would hear loud whispers as he walked down the school hallways, "Man, you hear about what happened to Smitty's mom?" The shame and embarrassment had followed him from school to school and he thought he had finally escaped the scandal and found peace. Angry, hurt, and depressed he quit attending school. My mother found out when she received a call from the school asking why James hadn't been attending. However, by that time, it was too late for him to graduate on time. He was going through one of the most crucial and pivotal stages in the life of a young Black male; a period of his life that would shape his life journey and he had no male role model to guide or advise him. He had no shoulder to cry on and had to carry that burden alone.

In the Spring of 1983, I finished fifth grade and we settled into our house in East Oakland. My mother required that we all work at the gift shop to earn our keep, including my sister Jai, when she came home from school in San Jose. We each received a crash course in business 101 and learned the fundamentals of running a business. There were mornings when we would rise at 5am to drive twenty minutes across the Bay bridge to San Francisco to purchase plants and flowers for the gift shop. The toll was only a dollar then. Some mornings we could see the shadow of the Golden Gate Bridge as the orange and yellow sun rose over the bay.

"The Town" in the eighties was a great place to grow up. Oakland was bustling with diversity and there was always something to do. The Oakland Coliseum was our playground. Communities had an abundance of recreational centers and sports programs in place to keep us kids engaged and stimulated. The streets in our neighborhood, as far as we were concerned, were safe enough to play on with no supervision until the streetlights came on. There were about eight of us kids playing on any given day, but sometimes as many as fifteen spending the day playing double dutch, stickball, singing, rapping, dancing, or just walking the tracks along San Leandro Boulevard to play at the Coliseum until they run us off.

We would enter local talent shows or put one on ourselves. During the summer we would practice day and night and right after school during the school year. None of us knew exactly what we were practicing for, but we knew we would be ready. Those were the good ol' days. When my sister Jai came to visit, she would play basketball at the school's hoop courts with my brother and the fellas from the neighborhood. Everyone would come watch this teen aged girl, school both boys her age and grown men on the court. It was truly something to see. My little cousin who would visit me at Mama's, would come to Oakland often and eventually lived with us for a little while, along with my god sister Netta. Netta is the younger sister of my brother's best friend Dewaine. She and my god brother's Tyrone and Jimmy who lived in our neighborhood are the children my mother helped to raise. She is a mother to so many to whomever needs her.

I attended McChesney Junior High School, now known as Edna M. Brewer Middle School and I must say, junior high was hella fun. Rap music was still in its infancy and being shaped and hip hop was becoming a culture. My school had some of the most talented people, many of whom went on to become doctors, lawyers, poets, musicians, chefs, activists and even a Grammy award winning artist. We were all so creative in our own unique way, and we were at a great school that for some of us, helped to enhance our talents and allowed us to display our craft. Sadly, by ninth grade, I would have to part with some of my friends due to the school district structure. Most of my classmates from the previous two or three years would be attending a different high school than me. My life made a huge turn after that.

Fremont High School is dead center in the middle of East Oakland on Foothill Boulevard. A good walking distance to the house I grew up in. While I was very self-confident, I was unsure of how to navigate the changing of a new school and meeting new people. It helped to have my best friend, who had also attended McChesney, there to soften the blow. Although we saw each other often and continued to be cool, we didn't hang out like we had. She and I had a few classes together, and eventually made new friends. Some days after school I would go to practice with my friend Trai who was a Dancer at the time for a popular Bay Area rap group, or I would go over to my sis Glenda's who had apartment up the street from the school on 55th and Foothill.

By my senior year I was too cool for school and singing was no longer a priority. I ignored sports and found no interest in art. My focus was on just being cool and "kickin' it" as we called it. I was too busy having fun to think about school and barely passing by my senior year. School wasn't hard for me; I just had no desire to attend. I did, however, enjoy my English Literature and Creative Writing classes. P.E. was held in the school auditorium while the gym underwent construction, so it was more like study hall. I cut that class a lot.

My mother had no idea I had been cutting class until it was too late, and I didn't have enough units to graduate on time just like my brother. I still participated in all the senior activities including Grad Nite at Disneyland, but I didn't walk the stage. I was embarrassed and my family was not happy. While some of my friends were preparing for college or heading to pursue their dreams after graduating. That summer I attended Laney College to earn a few units, but it still wasn't enough to graduate. As a result, my sister Jai, suggested to my mom that I come live with her in Stockton and that she would ensure that I graduated from high school. I was still seventeen when the fall semester began, so I was able to enroll at Franklin High School in Stockton, where I finished up the last few classes that I needed to walk the stage.

PART IV

Who is Jai?

I have always been proud to tell people that my sister Jai earned a four-year scholarship to San Jose State for basketball. She has always been head-strong, stubborn, and smart, just a natural athlete and a born leader. Some people are just born that way. But by the time I moved with my sister in the summer of 1990, she was thick in the game. She had gone from selling weed while in college playing basketball, to having withdrawn from school and was now on a whole other level on the streets of Stockton.

Jai was introduced to the game by one of our older cousins. She started selling weed because her "little job," as she called it, wasn't cutting it. As a condition of her scholarship, the NCAA didn't allow athletes to work until the off season, and the scholarship only covered so much. The scholarship primarily covered her tuition and books, with the rest of her expenses left to her and my mother to cover. My mother did what she could, and she thought my sister was still working during her off season. Jai was known for always having a job, sometimes two, and she saved her money well. During this time, I was in middle school, and when she got her own apartment and was no longer living on campus, Jai would come get me on the weekends. I knew she was selling weed, because I had seen the brown paper bags full of it, and as someone who was smoking weed, I knew what it was.

Jai never really came out to our family that she was gay. She'd always been a tom boy as far back as I could remember. My father would choose Pig sometimes, as he called her, over my brother to play football at the park when they were small. She hated dresses and loved Converse sneakers, jeans, and t-shirts. She always had a basketball in her hand and kept the company of pretty female friends. Although the family had suspected it for many years, no one ever questioned her. During a weekend visit to San Jose, she introduced me to her girlfriend - just like that! When I returned home from my visit, I told my mother, my sister, and my brother. It didn't matter to any of us. Our love was unconditional, and she was still my big sister and Mama's baby.

My sister knew that my mother needed assistance, securing things I required as a teenage girl. So, when I visited her in San Jose for the weekend, we would visit her friends, go out to eat, and she would take me shopping. When I returned home, my mom never really questioned the gifts because she assumed my sister was working. Jai had already completed three years of college, with only one more left to earn her B.A. The weekend before she withdrew from college, I visited Jai at school We did a lot of shopping that weekend and made many stops during the day which was always the norm. Before she took me home that Sunday, we made a stop to see her new Panamanian friend and a stop at the Adidas outlet where she practically bought me the store. As we loaded my haul into the back seat of her yellow Toyota Corolla, I thought to myself, "she's selling more than just weed." When I made it home and unloaded my stuff from the car, I'm certain my mother suspected that something was going on.

Jai caught her first case in 1987 for selling weed. After serving a few months in jail, she was released. She withdrew from school and moved back to Stockton where she would then be all in. Shortly after, during the summer of 1990, my mother allowed me to move with her, under the condition that I finished high school.

Always dressed, driving the tightest cars in town, and known for having a beautiful girl, Jai stayed on top of her game, and she was always paranoid. She could be heartless when it came to her money or her respect. Although the gangsters in our family had no problem putting hands on anyone who thought they could try her, she insisted on making sure that even without them she was not to be played with and could hold her own. She showed respect and love to those who gave her the same, and she was able to go into any neighborhood and hang or shoot dice. But I didn't know how deep in the game she was at the time.

There was always a party or a picnic to go to, and everybody would be out having fun or riding through. Stockton's hundred-degree heat didn't keep us inside, as there was always a porch to hang out on with some shade Uly's Store parking lot would be deep all day, and when one time came through, we'd just move across the street to Grand Save Market or run in Pop's yard on the corner. Cutie Pie Park stayed cracking, and everybody was getting money all over Stockton.

It was fun and exciting. I didn't understand the damage that was being done to our families, friends, and our people who were buying dope and getting high; how it would impact the community and the children of these families and friends that would have to grow up in this environment, long after we were gone and living our lives. We couldn't see it. It was all about getting money and looking good while you were doing it. Everybody was getting it or had a hustle. Crips, Bloods, and The MOB were constantly feuding with each other, and drive bys were a common occurrence out south. People were still dying and getting locked up all the time and that has never stopped.

That summer Jai bought me my first car. It was a 1969 Ford Falcon. My cousin Emmitt would drive me around in my car because I hadn't yet learned to drive. It was the first summer I lived in Stockton since my childhood. I was introduced to family that I hadn't seen since I was very young. It was fun being back in Stockton. Beautiful stary summer nights filled with the light chirps of crickets, and dry heat, occasionally met with a light delta breeze. Many of my cousins were my age, so we'd all get together at my sister's house and we'd party all day and all night. Jai was all about you having fun. Whatever your vice was, she'd have it in abundance for you and let you just have at it. Then she would put us to work. We would roll Vega's and Philly Blunts from bags full of weed. Then we were tasked with unfolding, organizing and counting endless trash bags full of money.

Cougars, candy paint, The Chronic, E40 and the Click. The 90's were full of good times and the parties were epic. People from all sides of town would come through just to get a peek inside the house party on Spring Street. No violence, just blocked streets filled with people and nowhere to park for blocks. Jai would spend a few thousand dollars on just beer and "drank" for the hood. Free forty's, gin and juice and Hennessy for those of us in the kitchen bartending. My best friend Reeshemah would be drinking Mad Dog 20/20 mixed Tahitian Treat or Hawaiian Punch. The party wouldn't end until the police arrived, got out of their cars, and cleared the street on foot. My big cousin who handled the door would quickly lock us in when he heard someone shout, "one-time comin!" We danced and partied til the wee hours of the morning, and nobody was worried about a job or they momma, cause they momma was prolly there too.

The day after the party, we would pay somebody to clean up the house. We were living in one of Granny's houses, and my Aunt who lived across the street, would often call Granny on us. Granny would drive from Madera bright and early Sunday morning, and we'd meet her at the gate. "I know y'all threw a party in my house an' had them streets blocked up with the po'lice." Of course, we'd deny it, and she'd tell us how she knew we were lying. "Ya'll throw one mo' party an' I gotta come back down here. I'm cutting thoats." My cousin CC stepped backwards and grabbed her throat, suggesting that she didn't want to be a victim. Granny eyed us as she walked back to get into her truck. Before she got in, she'd turn, and with her gold teeth gleaming, warned us "and I gotta nine-millimeter with a clip this long," her hands extended the length of a clip that they didn't even sell, and if they did, I'm sure it would be illegal. Granny was a piece of work, but we loved her to pieces.

Still in Oakland, my mom didn't have a clue of how deep things had become. She continued to work each day and we checked in regularly, keeping her updated on how we were doing. School was going well. I had bonded with my cousins who were going to school with me. I was on the honor roll. Back in choir again and I had enrolled in a photography class. Franklin was nothing like Fremont, but I liked it and I met some great people. By June of 1991, my sister had kept her promise to my mother, and I walked the stage and graduated from high school. After graduation, I got my own place in Stockton and a car that took me back and forth to Oakland.

I would help my mother at the gift shop in Oakland a few weekends each month, and the rest of my time was spent hanging and hustling in Stockton. That same year I became pregnant, and my sister Jai was livid. Eventually she got over it, and my beautiful daughter Saundria, was born in September of 1992. Just like my mother and my oldest sister Jamie, Jai would help me with her. She and my cousin CC would baby sit sometimes. When Saundria was about two years old, I banned them from tossing her back and forth between them across the room, regardless of how much my baby loved it.

By 1997, Jai was outta control and it was all coming to an end. She had already served time in prison for selling drugs, and her lawyer, whose kids she'd put through college with the money she paid him, suggested that she sit her ass down and end it. She moved to Oakland, not far from my mother but ended right back in Stockton about a year after she had arrived. She had almost been kidnapped in front of her apartment.

Not too long after that the feds came. They raided the seven homes of the people they claimed were major players in what they described as a cocaine ring with Jai being the ringleader. They showed up at Mama's house looking for money and whatever else they suspected my grandmother was holding. My uncle happened to be coming out of the house as they pulled up in a caravan of cars, search warrant in hand. He informed them that only his elderly mother was in the house and assured them that they didn't have to barge in the house or kick down the door. He offered to let them inside to search for whatever they were looking for. His priority was minimizing the trauma to Mama of a forceful search. They searched the house and found nothing but a few pictures.

When my mother received word about my sister being busted and the feds coming to Mama's, she was more disappointed than anything. As time had passed, she became aware of what my sister was doing, and she was never okay with it. With only a year left before she graduated, she was expected to be the first of my mother's children to earn her degree, ironically in Business. My mother's goal was that she to get a decent job and make good money the "right way" as she called it.

The morning after the raid, all of Stockton awoke to a front-page story in the Stockton Record which read:

A five-month investigation into a sophisticated drug ring ended Wednesday
with the arrests of 10 Stockton residents who reportedly were responsible
for distributing cocaine and rock cocaine throughout California and other
states, police said.
The investigation by the Combined Rural and City Narcotics Enforcement

Team and the Sacramento office of the Drug Enforcement Administration focused

on 31-year-old xxxxxx, whom police called the ringleader. Over the five months, investigators used undercover surveillance and

other techniques, such as buying drugs from the ring, to intercept a kilogram

(2.2 pounds of cocaine, 300 grams (10.5 ounces of rock cocaine and $54,000

in cash, said xxxxxx of the Sacramento DEA office. Investigators armed with search and arrest warrants from the U.S. Attorney's

Office in Sacramento stormed seven Stockton homes at 7 a.m. Wednesday and arrested J and nine others whom they are calling

major players in the ring.

"It's the magnitude of this operation. They weren't dealing grams.

They were dealing kilogram quantities," DEA Agent xxxx said.

(The above excerpt was taken from the Stockton Record archive)

None of our family were proud of what was reported in that story, except maybe my father. Not proud that she was locked up, but that she was such a major player. Her life filled with throwing epic parties, giving concerts, renting leer jets, and candy paint had come to an end. She would have to face the consequences of her actions. She had ignored the pleas of her attorney and our family to simply end it and walk away. She had made more than enough money to stop. My mother said, "the Lord had to sit her down, before she ended up dead or in prison longer than what she was sentenced too." The deeper you are in the game the more volatile and dangerous it becomes. Jai had become an altogether different person, a consequence of the lifestyle she had chosen. My sister was sentenced to fourteen years in a federal correction facility, serving most of her time in Dublin, California, with a three-year stint in Tallahassee, Florida. She was locked up with Heidi Fleiss, the Hollywood Madame,

Sara Jane Moore, who attempted to assassinate President Gerald Ford and a woman who had been sentenced to three consecutive life sentences plus twenty years for a drug offense but who was later granted clemency after twenty-three years, by President Barack Obama.

Shortly after her incarceration, I moved back to Oakland. We would visit Jai often and even Mama visited once or twice but seeing her baby in that environment was too hard for her. She didn't want to leave her there and she would cry. My mother faithfully made the thirty-minute drive to Dublin from Oakland each weekend. I told her that she served that time with my sister. Even while she was in Tallahassee, my mother was always on the phone with my sister. She ended up serving twelve years in prison of her fourteen-year sentence.

Once she was released, Jai had to start over from scratch and she was faced to confront all the scars that she had left behind. She returned to a new world, and everything was foreign to her. Cell phones looked different than when she left, and debit cards were a new thing. It was an intimidating adjustment to say the least. Before returning home, she spent some months in a halfway house. During her twelve years of confinement in those prisons, she had experienced so much, listened, and learned a lot; enough that it kept her from going back. Since she returned home, she has walked the straight and narrow, working a good job, earning great money, and living a respectable life born of the hard lessons she had learned.

I once asked her if she had made more than a million dollars during her time out there in the streets. She didn't want to answer, still carrying the regrets of her actions, but I insisted. Reluctantly, she answered that she had, "more than one," she said. She still doesn't like to talk about that period in her life and certainly doesn't glorify it. I believe that she feels tremendous guilt for the irreparable damage those activities inflicted on her people and the community. Very few of us contemplated what the lingering effects would be after the damage was done. When people ask me how she's doing I tell'um, "she's obeying all traffic signs and rules of the lan

The family is extremely proud of how she has turned her life around. She feels blessed that she is home with her family and friends. I'm hopeful that she will complete her last year of college and earn her B.A. in Business.

PART V

Broken & Restored

As painful as it has been to revisit many of the episodes from my life growing up, my family and I all agree that it has also been therapeutic. As I prepared to write this part of the book, I spoke with my oldest sister Jamie, who my dad called Cheeto, about the impact of events from our childhood and how they shaped the trajectory of her life. “The sins of our father shaped my life,” she said. “I took on a lot of what I saw while growing up.” We discussed bad relationship choices that she made, which were directly corelated to my parents’ relationship. What Jamie had seen my father inflict upon our mother, was preceded by the toxic treatment my mother had witnessed her father subject her mother to. She confessed to inheriting the family pathology of “not speaking up for myself and remaining quiet about things when I shouldn’t have. I want better for my life,” Jamie admits, “so I have to do better.”

My siblings and I have all coped differently with the sins of our parents. It was around 2004, while my middle sister Jai was serving time in prison and my brother James was about to move to Las Vegas with his family, that I was commuting back and forth between Oakland and Stockton and still trying to figure out my life. After near twenty years, my sister Jamie had been promoted to an executive position at the City of Oakland. She and my mother were becoming more involved with the church as well. Although Mama was raised in the church, she didn't attend much when she moved to California. Cha'ly didn't believe in it, and he had run Mama out of a revival at White Rose Church of God in Christ when my mother was a girl. Mama never went back to church after that. My mother, however, was allowed to go to church with the neighborhood kids, and she was eventually baptized. However, as she got older, she stopped attending too. We didn't attend church with my mother, and when we went to live with Mama, the most she would do was listen to Reverend Lonell Crosby, the "Old Gospel Traveler" on the local AM radio station, KSTN. She never discouraged us from attending church, though, and we sometimes went with friends. After my mother had been shot, she began attending church again more frequently and eventually we all did. But my sister Jamie wasn't as involved in church as my mother had become.

My mother had been looking for someone to clean her carpets and a friend of the family referred her to a local pastor who operated a cleaning service on the side. My mother called and scheduled an appointment to have her carpets cleaned. When the pastor arrived at the house to clean the carpets, he noticed a picture of Jamie. He asked my mother who was the young lady in the picture. Then questions suggesting his interest in meeting her. Some time passed and again, my mother scheduled an appointment to have him come again and clean the carpets. That time he was lucky enough that my sister was home. The two talked while he cleaned the carpets, and he was certain to say all the right things to her. Before he left, they exchanged numbers. Over the next few days, they talked regularly as he moved in quickly to secure his position as her new beau.

Jamie had been in a few bad relationships, the last of which, a four-year relationship with the perceived "Mr. Right," had ended about a year before. She wasn't seeking a sincere relationship, but she didn't want to put up a wall either and be closed from developing a healthy relationship. After a few dates with the pastor, things between them got serious and fast. He was the pastor of a church in Oakland and she was quickly introduced to people in his inner circle, his children, and members of his church. She recalled, "I was just starting to learn about church." Everything seemed okay in the beginning. The people she met were all nice and receptive of her. She would spend time together with his family and attend his church events. He was very attentive and available.

Less than a year after they began dating, he proposed. She enthusiastically accepted and a wedding date was set. Over two hundred-fifty people were to be invited and the extravaganza was to be held at one of the biggest churches in Oakland. Ten bridesmaids, ten groomsmen, five flower girls, two ring bearers, and a partridge in a pear tree. The church, flowers, dresses, cake, and photographer had all been paid.

Family had contributed time and money into this anticipated event. The bridal shower was beautiful and all that remained was the wedding. Without warning, a week before the wedding, Jamie's fiancé became sick and was unable to proceed. The bridal party and invited guests were advised that the wedding was placed on hold until further notice. Jamie hadn't shared, that problems had been brewing for some time before the proposal. From the dysfunctional co-parenting situation with his children's mother, to an ex-girlfriend who wouldn't go away, to some new chick who claimed that she too was in a relationship with the pastor. I had long suspected that something about him wasn't genuine. From day one he seemed like a faker.

About a month after the wedding was indefinitely postponed, I received a call from a family friend who was member of his church. He informed me that the pastor had sold the church from up under the congregation, had taken all the money and left. Though he had left the church, he remained in Oakland, living his life as if he had done nothing wrong. The members of the church were devastated. My sister hadn't been aware that he had done any of this, and when she did find out, he told her some outlandish story that was good enough for her to continue seeing him.

After having stolen the church's money and the new chick unexpectedly showing up more than he wanted, things were getting hot in Oakland for the pastor. He suggested that he and Jamie move to Las Vegas to get a fresh start. So, my sister packed her things, gave notice to her employer of over twenty years, and left her executive position for the uncertainty of life in Las Vegas. They found an apartment in Summerlin, and she quickly found a job providing legal office support. He was banking on a position at a local church. At the time, my brother James and his family, as well as my nephew's mom Twyla, who is like a sister to us, had been living in Las Vegas for quite some time. We were comforted knowing that she had family there to support her. My nephew spent a lot of time with Jamie which made her very happy. She would go to the hair salon almost every week, where his mom worked, to have her hair done. Sometimes she would just hang out with the girls at the salon to pass time. She was struggling to adjust, and I could tell that she was missing us and California.

One day we received a call that Jamie and her fiancé had decided to get married in Las Vegas. A handful of our family packed up and headed to Las Vegas for the second try at their previously postponed wedding. My brother James and the groom went to pick up their tuxedos and while there, the groom again comes down with another mysterious illness. An ambulance was dispatched and whisked him to the hospital. In the chaos of the moment, no one thought to cancel the limo, which arrived at James' to pick us up. Of course, there was no bride and no groom, as the groom had been admitted to the hospital with my sister by his side. A few days later, we all returned to California, still no wedding. It was clear that he was stalling, and it was obvious that he had no intentions of getting married.

The phone calls from the new chick to their home phone and his cell phone hadn't stopped. One morning Jamie answered the house phone, and it was the chick saying he had been lying to them both. She stated that he had told her that he lived alone in Las Vegas, and each time she mentioned that she was coming to visit him, he would quickly arrive at her door in Oakland. "He's a liar and he never had intentions of marrying you," she told my sister. After that heated conversation, my sister confronted him about the allegations and he, of course, denied it all.

The churches in Las Vegas wouldn't touch him with a ten-foot pole so he began searching for work outside of Las Vegas. They'd been there for about four months and the calls between my sister and I became fewer and shorter when we did talk. One day I received a call from

Twyla in Las Vegas asking if I had talked to Jamie. I told her that it had been a few days and that she had seemed preoccupied when we spoke. She said told me that she hadn't been to the salon in over a week, not even to get her hair done. My nephew had been calling her and she wasn't answering. I knew in that moment that something was wrong. I immediately called my brother and he confirmed that he hadn't heard from her either. Worried, I called her, and luckily, she answered. She didn't sound well. She sounded very weak and down in the dumps. Although I tried, nothing I said made her laugh or cheered up. She insisted that nothing was wrong, but I knew better.

After we hung up, I called my mother in tears and told her what was going on. I told her that I'd be taking a few days off from work to go see about my sister. The next day my daughter and I jumped on a plane, headed to Las Vegas. My sister picked us up from the airport and my daughter was elated to see her. She missed her auntie who had always been a second mother to her. We both noticed that she looked tired and had lost a lot of weight, likely the result of stress and not eating. Her coke bottle figure was gone. She was now just a frail and fragile frame. Her fiancé was at the apartment when we arrived, but I didn't speak to him. He quickly left and didn't come back until after we had returned to California. Her apartment was spotless, but dark and empty. After settling into the guest bedroom, we returned to the living room to hang out. We laughed, talked, and snacked out while watching movies. Later that evening, she made a lasagna with garlic bread, and a green salad.

That night, after my daughter had fallen asleep, my sister and I had a sister-to-sister talk. She shared with me that he was hardly ever at the apartment, and that she was there alone most of the time except for occasions when my nephew came to visit. She said she felt deserted and her spirit dry like the desert she was living in. She added that the chick had never stopped calling and harassing her. I hurt for her and felt helpless because I couldn't help her out of the situation that she was in. It wasn't my call. All I could do was be there and give her the best advice any sister would which was to "leave his ass!" We cried and talked ourselves to sleep that night. The next morning after breakfast, before she dropped us off at the airport, I begged her to just come back to California and start over. She said that she would. But she needed to close out a few things before she left. Las Vegas had become too stressful, and she missed home.

A month had passed, and Jamie still hadn't come home. Her fiancé claimed that he'd been asked to pastor a church in Fresno. He said the church would provide a house for him to live in, but Jamie couldn't stay with him because it wouldn't look right that they were living together and not yet married. He said he would be there primarily on the weekends to preach, until they found a place of their own to share in Fresno. He assured her that they would still be married when the time was right. His promise to only be in Fresno on the weekends to preach proved to be a lie. She was lucky if she saw him a few times a month. She drove up and down the 99 to the 15 highways weekly, between Las Vegas, Fresno. The I-5 to the 280 between Oakland and Stockton, chasing behind him and trying to find a place to live.

I was now living in Stockton and my mom had also moved back to Stockton to take care of Mama who was now in her late eighties. One night, my sister called my mom to say she would be there shortly. The doorbell rang and when she opened the door to let her in, my mom saw the red taillights of a vehicle turning the corner as the pastor drove away. He hadn't even waited for Jamie to get inside the house before he had drove off. She was dehydrated, malnourished and stress had overtaken her. He had dropped my sister off and he never came back. "It was heartless," my mother said.

The next morning was a beautiful day. The sun was shining bright, and the birds were chirp-chirp-chirpin.' My mother called and told me what had happened the night before. I got dressed and rushed over to see my sister. I parked in front of the house and as I made my way to the front door, the smell of smothered potatoes and onions escorted me in. I could see the shadow of my mom approaching the entry way. As she opened door, she sighed in disgust and said, "she's in there, in the room." The bedroom was dark with all the blinds closed and the television off. She was clearly not in a good space. I opened the blinds and cheerfully said "good mornin," though my heart was hurting for her. The anger I felt for that man had my blood boiling and my stomach churning. "Get up and let's go get some fresh air," I said. But she was embarrassed, too weak, and sick to her stomach to get up. I sat on the edge of her bed and talked with her for a while. Eventually, she got the energy to sit up to eat, but quickly laid back down.

A few days later, stressed and not eating, Jamie was rushed to the hospital, where she would remain for about two weeks until she had regained enough strength to return home. My father, who was living in Fresno at the time, got a ride to Stockton to be with my sister. Although Jamie and my father would talk once or twice a week, she had never discussed what she was going through with the pastor or the drama between her the chick. My father was unable to keep his own life on track, so how could she expect him to give her the sound advice, or guidance that she would need from her father. Hell, we were always babysitting him when we were with him. My father seeing Jamie hospitalized was a wakeup call for him, even if it was short lived. My mother said when he arrived at the hospital he was speaking clearly and making plenty of sense. He told my mother to go home and get some rest and that he would handle it from there, and he did. He was there by her side every day until her release. He clearly hadn't been drinking as much, and had a lot to marinate on while there at the hospital with her.

My dad had assured us that Jamie was his first born. How true that is, is still unknown. But, if you ask any of my mom's children who was my father's favorite, we'd all answer "Jamie." As he got older, Jamie was the only one who could get him in line when he was acting up, and she is the only one of my mother's children that has pictures with him. None of the rest of us have photos with him when we were kids that I am aware of.

Once Jamie was released from the hospital and was well and on her feet, my dad was back cuttin' up again and Jamie realized that her old life as an executive was over. She had to start from scratch. Dude had drained the 401K that she had worked twenty-three years to build. Her things had been placed in a storage unit in Fresno in his name and she was only able to reclaim less than half of her belongings. He kept her artwork, her CD's, her movie collection, and many personal items of value. She found church no longer as appealing, as it had been for the many years that she had been a Christian. She had begun to doubt her faith in the Lord. She wasn't praying or reading the Word as she had always faithfully done. Her faith was broken. After of few months back in Stockton and trying to wrap her head around how the hell she got back there, she began attending a local church with my mother. Gradually, she began attending Bible study, volunteering at the church, and ultimately attended a church retreat that started to rebuild her faith. She began to pray and read the Word again.

She was also still searching for a job, and the harsh reality was that she was no longer in the Bay Area anymore. She was back in Stockton and the pay was nowhere close to what she had been earning two years earlier. It didn't matter though, she had to start somewhere. The church hired her as a receptionist and five years later, she was promoted to administrative assistant. It was a different world than what she was accustomed too. But she went for it head on and did her job well, keeping her work skills sharp and honed for the next plan God had in store for her. She worked with great people who became part of our family. They cared for her, loved, and nurtured her and helped to build her back up just as we did. Some of the staff and church members knew her story, while others didn't.

Seven and a half years had passed, and her health had improved, and her mind, body and spirit were all in a good place. She had met new people and rekindled old friendships from her youth. She was smiling and happy most of the time. But she still bore the scars of having been hurt and mistreated and suffering the loss of everything she'd worked so hard for. It wasn't that she didn't appreciate what Stockton had given her, but there was something missing. She missed Oakland. Her life there as an executive, the hustle and bustle, the culture, the people, jus "The Town" in general. It was her city as she called it, but that season of her life had run its course; it was over. At times, thinking about it would bring her spirit down, but our family always found a way to pull her back up. It was a hard pill for her to swallow. But even those days got easier, and we continued to pray and have faith.

Jamie continued to keep in touch with a few of her former Oakland co-workers and friends, and she was invited to an investiture's ceremony for a former co-worker who was being sworn in as a judge. She was reluctant to go, but after some thought and words of encouragement from my mother, she decided to attend.

She hadn't seen many of these people in over seven years, and she was uncertain of how she would be received. When she arrived at the ceremony and slowly approached the entry way, she was nervous. Her fears, however, were quickly calmed as she was greeted with smiles and hugs from coworkers and friends who were happy to see her and had missed working with her. She had a wonderful time that afternoon. While at the event, Jamie caught the attention of an amazing woman who would change her life in an instant. They had worked together years before and she was familiar with my sister's professionalism, character, and work ethic. She was looking for an executive to work with her and believed Jamie would be the perfect person for the job. She asked would she be interested in coming back to work for her in the same capacity that she had worked before. Before Jamie could answer, she suggested that she apply for the position. Immediately after leaving the ceremony, Jamie and my mother called me to share the news. I could hear the excitement in her voice; an excitement that I hadn't heard from her in a long time. She told me what happened, and I was so happy for her. It was as if she had already secured the job. We prayed on the phone and later she applied for the position.

Every day for weeks, I would ask if she'd heard anything about the job, and finally the day came when it was confirmed that she had been offered the job. Same job, same executive job title, same office, and same phone number. Of course, the church didn't want her to leave, but they were proud and happy for her. It had been a long journey. With prayer, faith, patience, and forgiveness-she made it. She had been restored.

She told me, "The Bible says, seven years is completion, eight years is a new beginning." She had been employed at the church for seven and a half years. She returned to her job in Oakland eight years after she had left. She purchased a new car – a Genesis, which represented her new beginning.

Jamie

Me & Saundria at Granny's House in Madera, California (1996)

PART VI

My Mission

I have two beautiful daughters who are seventeen years apart in age. My oldest daughter, Saundria, aka Sunny or Sunny Bunny, was born one month before my nineteenth birthday. I wasn't even legally old enough to purchase alcohol or get into clubs yet. Her father and I dated off and on until she was about five years old, when it became just me and her. My mother and my sisters helped me a lot, as did her dad's mother, when she could. I had both a job and a hustle. I was blessed to have people in my life who genuinely loved on my baby during a time where I had no clue of what it took to raise a little girl, as I was still a baby myself. Although I was in Stockton and my mother was living in Oakland, my mother stayed in my business and was always present. Saundria and I had our own place and she had everything she could want or need, or so I thought. My mother understood that I was still young and wanted to go out and live. She had also been a teen mother, and both Mama and Granny helped her, so she paid it forward and helped me.

Even though I had village who helped me with her my mother still made me responsible for my child, at a time when I didn't want to be. She didn't know I was selling weed, but she made it clear that I had better be working or in school. So, I kept a job of some sort and kept hustling-strictly greenery though.

When my sister Jai got busted, shit got real. Although I continued to work and hustle, I realized that we needed a change because the streets were changing too. The game wasn't the same, and the environment in which I was operating wasn't the best for raising a little girl. Her father was about to sentenced to several years in prison and I needed to create a better life for us, so I decided to move back to Oakland with my four-year-old to live with my mother. My mother was still in the same house, still owned the Gift Shop, and worked another part time job. My sister Jamie and my aunt Brenda were living with her too, both working for the City of Oakland. Everyone was doing something positive and moving in a productive direction...except me, so something had to change. It was nice being back in "The Town." It had changed a lot, but the good vibe was still there.

I was starting over, so I was on a mission to do better, and I did. I enrolled my daughter in a good preschool and got to it. I was accepted into Saint Mary's College paralegal program which was a new extended law studies program. During my last semester, I landed a job as a document clerk at a law firm where I would work part time until I finished the program. The firm was about twenty minutes from the campus, in the city of Walnut Creek. My mother, my sister, and my aunt would help care for my baby, and she loved being with them.

After I completed the paralegal program, I secured an even better position in the Saint Mary's College Law Studies department as an Administrative Assistant. I was the only Black person in that office, and from what I was told, no one could remember anyone Black having ever working in that department there before. The law firm where I had worked part-time was no better. There was only one Black male attorney working there when I started, with a second being hired by the time I left. I had worked there for almost five years, and even though I had completed my internship there and received my paralegal certification, they wouldn't hire me. They always had an excuse: "we're hiring a paralegal, but not an entry level." There was too much bullshit, a lot of driving, and more time away from my daughter. Saint Mary's paid well, but it wasn't what I had gone to school for.

After twenty-three years, my mother closed the doors of her Gift Shop and moved back to Stockton to be closer to Mama. My aunt Brenda had also moved back to Stockton. So, guess what I did? I moved back too. I had interviewed for a legal assistant position for a family law attorney in Midtown Sacramento, about forty miles north of Stockton, and I killed the interview. I was offered the job, given a start date, a job title, and I quickly submitted my resignation to my current employers. Since deciding to leave Oakland, I had been scouting apartments and schools and figured Sacramento would be the perfect place for me and my daughter to make another fresh start. Sacramento isn't too country or too city. It gives you just enough of both, and I'd be thirty minutes from my family.

Well as the saying goes, "man plans and God laughs" because while everything had fallen in place, I received a fax at my current office from the new employer who I was to begin working for in a few days, stating that they had changed their mind about hiring me and wished me the best of luck. I tried calling but I was placed on hold until eventually I hung up. I was able to submit the fax I had received to the unemployment office which allowed me to receive benefits until I found a job. I was crushed though and felt as if I was falling backwards. At that point, I questioned why I had left Oakland in the first place.

I was pissed when I found myself back at the temp agency in Stockton that had previously sent me out on odd clerical jobs. This time around, I was assigned a job working for a bankruptcy attorney who, during that assignment, I only met twice. Our first meeting was at the interview. He hired me and left the key to the office with the building's doorman and sent me an email with instructions of what he needed me to do, which included answering the phones, opening mail, and responding to correspondence. I only worked for him for about 2 weeks before the assignment ended. I was growing increasingly more frustrated, but I didn't give up, Thankfully, my family continued to rock with me through it all. The last call that I received from the temp agency would be a game changer. The offer was a temp to hire position working for the Port District. At that point I was no longer concerned that it wasn't a legal position. I just needed a stable job with good benefits and a 401K. For three months I worked as a document assistant before applying for a clerk position in another department which offered more pay, full benefits, and that coveted 401K.

My daughter had reached the fifth grade and she hated Stockton. She wanted us to go back to Oakland; back to the school that she had attended since kindergarten. As a parent I did what I thought was the best move for us both, not considering how that change would affect her socially and emotionally. I was the momma and she had to do what I said. I rented a nice little two-bedroom duplex. She had a cool room, nice clothes, and plenty of converse. I took her on trips to Disneyland, to the Teen Choice Awards. She had cells phones, a sewing machine for her fashion projects, and whatever else she needed or desired. She still had her Granny (my mother), and all her cousins, uncles, and aunts. But I had to work just as my mother had, so emotionally I wasn't as available to her as I should have been. Since birth, she was always a very content child, never making much of a fuss about anything. She didn't cry much and didn't require anyone in her face all the time. Her philosophy seemed to be feed me, love on me, let me sleep and leave me be. She was just always a good kid. So, I just always assumed that she was fine. When in fact she needed more of my attention than what I was giving It was an unaware selfishness. But, the love for my child was always there.

Saundria's relationship with her father was still non-existent even after his return home from prison. His family, however, was always loving and available to her. By the time she was in 10th grade I had a failed attempt at marriage which lasted about four years and after that Saundria and I started to adjust to our little world of just us. Things were steadily coming together, and my next objective was to buy a house, which I did. Work was great, I was getting promotions, earning more money, and accruing sick and vacation hours. I was twenty-nine years old and finally had a real, damn job with stability and benefits.

I told myself that I wouldn't get too comfortable, and I'd eventually pursue legal work again. Saundria was starting to meet new friends and became involved in band at school. However, she still would struggle with most things teenage girls do in High School. Trying to find out who she is, dealing with friends, boys, and just life. She also, wanted a better relationship with not only her dad, but also with me.

So, while Saundria and I were settling into our new life, I met someone who I really had no intention of building a relationship with. He was young, fine, great body, and he caught my eye. He was also able to keep my attention. In my mind, I wasn't ready for a relationship, as I was focused on my mission. But we had a true connection and dated for about a year before ultimately breaking up. It just didn't work out, I guess.

Now in her mid-eighties, Mama was getting older, and the family was concerned about her living alone. She had already burnt her hand trying to cook and had completely ignored using her life alert monitor after a previous incident where she had alerted them by accident. It was clear that she didn't need to be living alone. However, she had no plans to leave her home either. My mother, now living in Stockton, not too far from Mama, decided that after Mama's next doctor appointment she would get her to spend the night with her and see how it went from there. After a few days passed at my mother's house, I think Mama had a feeling she wouldn't be returning to her home. She wasn't sad or upset though as she had plenty of company and most of her personal things were brought to my mother's so she could feel close to home.

Each day different family members would drop by to see Mama. We continued to have family gatherings and birthday parties as we had always done. I would come over on some Sundays and cook her breakfast while my mom went to church. We would talk like we had when I was a little girl. She would share with me things she had seen during her lifetime. She was amazed by the cell phone and its capabilities. She recalled how she would write letters to communicate with family and friends and it would take months for the letter to reach the person. Instead of simply picking up the phone and directly dialing a person, she would call the operator who had to connect her to the person she wanted to speak to. "and, what are they doing to these chickens?" she asked, "cause chicken wings shouldn't be that little." She never thought she'd see the day where the United States would elect a black president either. She thought he was handsome too.

Mama didn't talk as much as she used too, but she still loved the company of family, and she was a great listener. I'd get her to laugh, and she would say a few things here and there, but she would tire quickly. She'd nod off and I would make sure she was comfortable. I was honored to be able to take care of her as she had cared for me. After some years and a few hospitalizations, Mama passed away at the age of ninety-one. Uncle Bufford now in his early eighties had come to visit when she last got hospitalized and didn't leave until after her funeral. He stayed at my mother's house about a month.

The devastation of Mama's passing woke me up in a way that shook me to my core. I had never experienced death on that level; someone who was that close to me. When I got the news that morning, I went numb. Saundria was at my mother's house, and I was home alone. I didn't cry right away. The emotions would come and go like it wasn't real, but when I did cry, it was hard and pitiful. My sister Jai was still serving the last few weeks of her prison sentence. Her greatest fear had been realized; that Mama would pass before she finished her time in prison. I was in no condition to drive, but I knew that I had only an hour and a half to make it to the Dublin prison to see my sister before the end of visitation that day. I thought about how close she was to coming home and the loneliness of her having no one to mourn with. Her heart would surely break with no one there to hug her. Someone needed to be there to support her.

I jumped on the freeway and darted to Dublin. I arrived two minutes too late to sign in. The prison staff wouldn't allow me to visit, even after informing them of our grandmother's passing. As expected, my sister took it hard, but her friends were there to support her. The loss was rough for my entire family, and my stress was at an all-time high. I had been basking in the fruit of my hard work. I had been attending church more, I had purchased a new house, achieved financial stability, gained a new outlook on life, and my daughter was adjusting to the changes. It was great, until I lost Mama. I was down and depressed and her passing took me a while to get back to the old me. But I had to be okay for not only me, but my Saundria. Three weeks before the first anniversary of Mama's death, my father suffered a stroke and slipped into a coma. In an effort to keep my light shining, I did a lot of praying and stayed surrounded by positive people. Family continued to be my rock.

While praying at my father's hospital bedside that he would make it out of the coma, I received an unexpected call from that fine young man who I had once dated. He called to check on me after finding out that my father was in a coma. After we hung up, we talked again the following day. On the third day Malcolm was in Fresno with me, where he remained until my father passed away. He has never left my side since.

I became pregnant with my second daughter soon after we got back together, and our daughter was born the following year on Valentine's Day. The summer after our baby was born, we were married on a beautiful beach in Pacifica, California. We shared that breathtaking view with about one hundred of our family and friends. My favorite picture from that special day shows us jumping the broom. We've been married for nine years and together for fourteen. We have enjoyed many ups and weathered the downs, but we are still together.

Named after her grandparents **Me**lvin and **Lo**is, **Ja**mes and A**lice**. I was thirty-nine when I gave birth to my daughter Melo Ja'lice and when she was about three

Melo Ja'lice - Kauai, HI (2017)

years old, I became a full-time stay at home Mom. She has a spicy personality, but very sweet. Raising her is so different than my experience raising Saundria. I am now able to volunteer at her school. I take her to basketball practice, basketball games, workouts, and field trips and in between being a mom, I find time to drop off the dog at the groomer and of course grab a "fro-yo." Yes, I am now that mom.

I still carry feelings of guilt because I didn't have time to be more available to Saundria because I was a young mother, working and kickin' it a lot. However, she and I have always remained close and we talk all the time. She's the best big sister ever. She recently expressed to me that she felt invisible and unseen by me during most of her childhood; that I didn't listen to her when she needed me to. She said she heard from me too many times that she shouldn't feel a certain way because she had everything she needed and more and that she should be grateful. That led her not to speak up because she felt she wasn't being heard anyway. She told me that she understood that I was young and doing the best I could, that she loves me and that "I've already been forgiven Mom." Her feelings were true and real, and in my face. We cried and shared, and I apologized, and we hugged some more. I cautioned her to learn from the mistakes that I had made with her, and to avoid doing the same with her own kids. My mission was to keep her safe, and to provide for her physical needs, while still showing her that I loved her. Unfortunately, this resulted in me providing more materially and being less emotionally available to listen to her feelings. I wish I had made more time to simply hold her a little bit longer.

Acknowledging my shortfalls was freeing for me and for her. It was a talk that we were destined to one day have as I didn't want her to carry those unnecessary burdens which may cause her a lifetime of emotional stress. I try not to make the same mistakes in how I raise her younger sister. But my mindset and outlook on life is completely different this time around. My life and its pace, along with my interests are all different. I'm truly blessed to be able to stay home and be a mom, which is a hard job too. God is good. Life is good, and I can't complain. I have two beautiful and talented daughters, an amazing husband, and a family who enrich my life. Priceless.

PART VII

My Poppa was a Rolling Stone

As a child, my only recollection of my father is of him dressed in his brown and yellow PG&E uniform with a neat afro. But ask anyone else who knew him back in the day, and they will tell you that he stayed dressed from head to toe. His fingernails were manicured and his 'fro was tight at all times, an image of my father I had never seen. My first impression of him after having not seeing him for about twelve years was not so good. He didn't stink, but he looked very unkept, and stayed that way most of the time. He wore a purple tam on his head that covered twigs of hair that peeked from underneath. His face was still smooth, but he had a knot on his forehead that needed attention, which he ignored for years until he finally had it removed. He was no longer using drugs, as far as I knew, but he still drank a lot, smoked cigarettes like a train, and had bad feet - mainly because his shoes were too small. His students from the college where he taught would give him shoes, so he rarely bought his own. His mustache was so long, and he'd joke that he was storing left over beer in it for later. He was calm and seemed a bit embarrassed, but after we talked and I was able to express to him how I felt, we were good. It didn't matter to me how he was dressed or what he looked like, he was my daddy, and I was going to love on him and allow him to do the same. I was able to forgive him, and not allow his mistakes lead me down a destructive path. After that reunion, my sister Jamie and I became as much of a part of his life as we could for the last twenty plus years of his life.

When my brother James was in his early twenties, he went to live with my father. Life in Oakland had become a bit overwhelming, given the negative influences and no male guidance. My father was teaching at a university and living in nice sized two-bedroom apartment across from the school. His first night there, my brother shared that he stood over my father with a knife and contemplated killing him, just as my father had attempted to kill my mother years before. He replayed in his mind the hurt, pain and dysfunction that my father had inflicted on his family. Stabbing him to death would make it right. Thoughts of how that decision would impact the lives of my mother and his sisters stopped him from following through. But it wouldn't be the only night that he would stand over my father's drunken body, ready to gut him like a fish.

While there, the two would often visit my Granny in Madera, which was only thirty minutes away. She would cook and fuss over my brother. However, the relationship between my father and my brother was closer to that of college roommates. They partied hard and had a good time, but my father avoided opportunities to forge the father/son bond my brother had longed to have. One evening, while alone at the apartment, my brother struck up a conversation that my father found uncomfortable. He told my brother that he had to go to the school to finish up some work. When my brother offered to join him, my father told him that only students and faculty were allowed at the school which my brother knew to be a lie considering that we had all visited the school many times up until the day he retired.

Not long after my father left the apartment, my brother James arrived at the school which infuriated my father. With no students or faculty present, my brother lost it. He yelled that my father was incapable of accepting love. He said he was tired of trying to win my father's attention and affection. James headed back to the apartment and packed his things. When my father returned to the apartment, my father apologized but there wasn't much of an exchange between the two. My father was incapable of going deep. He didn't know how to be a father and have those much-needed conversations.

It wasn't long before James headed back to my mother in Oakland, and we were all happy to have him home. The band was all back together again. My mother had never spoken negatively about my dad until we were adults and sharing our own grievances. We all had a chance to see and experience who he really was for ourselves.

It was tough for James being back in "The Town" as it had changed a lot in just a few short years. Oakland had no mercy, and it was easy to get caught up even when doing all the right things. As a young man, James made some bad decisions but he made it through. He found a good job where he met his amazing wife and they have been married over twenty-five years. They have four amazing children.

Before my sister Jai went to prison, she wanted no parts of our father. He would try and call her from time to time, but she really didn't want to talk. When she did answer the phone, out of respect she'd hold a piece of a conversation, while Jamie and I would talk to him a few times a week. There were periods, however, when we would not hear from him for a few weeks. But we could usually reach him by phone in his classroom at the university where he worked when school was in session. It was a lot of work trying to track him down, and at times we would worry. It was like having an irresponsible son in college. He lived in a weekly motel while school was in session, but when he was on semester break, he'd check out of the motel and ride trains all over California until school started back. He was known as Hobo Jim, and he thought this was so cool. We thought it was crazy and dangerous. He was an educated man, teaching at a university. He had a home to go to and yet he chose to live like he did. It was crazy.

He had finally got settled in an apartment a few years before he passed, with a piano in the living room that he would play all the time. He called me one morning at 2am, drunk. I could hear him playing the piano in the background. "Baby, I wrote a song called Sweet Alice," and he began to sing and play a song about my mother. Half asleep, I listened, and when he had finished, I said, "that's nice Daddy, I'll call you in a couple hours." We hung up after saying I love you, but he didn't answer the phone when I tried calling back later that morning. That wasn't the first or the last time that he would have those moments of sadness. He was punishing himself for what he had done, not only to my mother and to us, but his other children that he had left behind. We met a few women he had dated during those years, but he never remarried. He told me and my sister Jamie, "your mother was a good woman, and I messed up."

Some years before reconciling with my father, I had learned that I had another brother L who was born in between my brother James and my sister Jai. My father had been seeing his mother while with he was with my mother. We went to watch him play basketball at Alameda College, and over time we formed a great relationship. I would visit him from time to time when I was in Stockton. He was always kind and protective. It was good times hanging out with him and his girlfriend who was Twyla at that time. My brother James stayed with them for a while too.

One weekend during the summer while in Madera at Granny's house, I asked my father if he had other kids besides the five of us and he answered honestly that he did. "There are about ten more," he said. He listed cities and states from all over, including Stockton and Hawaii. Two of the ten were twin boys who lived in Bakersfield. He admitted to getting one of his students at the university pregnant and said that she had given birth to his boys, who he talked about all the time. Her parents were furious and would not allow my father to see the twins. The twins' mother would sneak behind her parents back and allow my father to see them a few times a year. My father got older and despite my request to meet them, the time never seemed right.

The week before my father passed, he called me. "Baby, you gone be proud of me, I haven't had a drink or a cigarette in three days." I told him that I was very proud and knew that he could do it. "I love you Daddy. I'll call you in the morning." That was the last time I spoke with him. It wasn't unusual for my dad not to answer his phone for days, but eventually he would call. About a week had passed when one morning as Jamie was rushing out of the door for work, she received a call from Kaiser Permanente in Fresno. They asked if she knew a James Smith. According to the person on the other end of the phone, my father had been admitted to the hospital and was on life support. He had come to the hospital a few nights before and was admitted. While there, he suffered a stroke, hit his head on the floor and fell into a coma. After a few days and no one having called looking for him, my sister was contacted as she was his only known contact. Initially, the hospital staff thought my father was a transient because of how he looked. Jamie and I rushed to Fresno, where we remained for ten long days.

Our days were shared with family and friends who came to offer their prayers and show their love and support. My Aunt OD's son, one of my father's closest cousins and like a brother to him, was right there with us until my father drew his last breath. I made a small collage that I hung in his room, full of old and new photos of him and his family, as well as photos of his artwork which were displayed at the University and in the Downtown City Park. Some photos displayed his exceptional achievements in basketball and football. The hospital staff was floored by his talents and accomplishments, and we were there as proof that he existed and was loved regardless of his past mistakes.

My mother, the woman who he married, abused, and shot, was there with him, rubbing his feet on his death bed. She'd forgiven him a long time ago and reminded him of that as she wiped his brow. My sister Jai, the daughter who had refused to forget the hurt and pain that he caused her, and her family finally arrived three days before his transition. She had no desire to see the man who had been nothing but mean to her as a child but my oldest daughter, in high school at the time, asked her to go see him for her, and she did. He had never shed a tear or showed any emotion during those eight days. He laid there still, helpless, and almost lifeless. His feet too long for the bed he was lying in. Jai walked over to him and grabbed his hand and said into his ear, "it's me, it's Pig," and tears began to roll down his face. He didn't say a word. He didn't have too. I knew he was sorry. He had communicated his regrets to me several times. He knew that he had ruined a great family. He would tell me often, "Baby, God gone leave me here to watch all the people that I love go before me." I'd tell him that I didn't believe God wanted him to suffer like that. I had forgiven him, and my mom had too. I encouraged him to go on with his life and live the best he could. But that never happened, and his children were left to pick up the pieces of what he left behind.

One of his girlfriends, Yolanda, who my siblings and I had known for long time was there with us almost every day. She was the first woman, after my parents broke up, that we would see when we'd visit him in Madera and Fresno. She was nice to us and regardless of how he had treated her, she still loved him, and she was there for him. She was supportive of us as well, while he lay in a coma. She said that her grandson wanted to come visit and asked would it be okay. We welcomed him, and when he arrived, he was all broken up. He shared with us that my father had raised him and his kids since he could remember. It sounded like my father was good to them, and they all loved him. He referred to my Father as "Paw-Paw" and his children did as well. He upset and confused though. He didn't know who we were, and why he had never heard about us. He looked at the collage on the wall and asked, "is that him?" I answered yes. He was just as heartbroken as everyone else my father had hurt. Hurt by my father's lies and deceit, but he still loved him for the time and love he had invested in him and his kids. He had never known that my father once had a wife and family, other children, or played pro-ball. After his visit and the history lesson about his "Paw-Paw," he asked if we would keep him posted on my father's condition. We hugged him with understanding and love and agreed that we would.

Yolanda remained at the hospital praying and weeping over the man who broke her heart and cheated on her with various women, just as he had with my mother. She warned us that another woman my father had been seeing, Diamond, might call and she did. Diamond called three times that day, crying, cussing, high out of her mind, and claiming that she was coming to the hospital to see him. That she was pissed off that other women were there with him on his death bed and she wasn't. She said she needed to get into his place to get her shit. Those calls were pure chaos and my sister, and I refused to entertain it. Before I ended the last call, I informed her that it wasn't in her best interest to come to that hospital. We were his kids, and she was not permitted anywhere near him.

We continued to pray, and my father's cousin and my husband Malcolm were our rocks. The doctor came in to explain that my father was no longer breathing on his own and that it was the machine breathing for him. Decisions needed to be made. We decided to take him off the machine and as the hours passed his oxygen level lowered. Malcolm and I left the hospital to take a break, and after about thirty minutes I got a call from my sister telling me to come back. We got back to the hospital and ran up the staircase to the ICU. I walked into the room, drew back the curtain back to see my father's cousin pacing and reciting the 23rd Psalm: "as I walk through the valley of the shadow of death, I will fear no evil." As my sister and Yolanda cried, I could see his oxygen levels plummet on the monitor. I grabbed his hand and said "Daddy, I love you," and with that he exhaled his last breath...and the monitor sounded the flatline alert. He was gone. The nurses rushed into the room but from there on, everything is a big blur. He passed away on May 5, 2010.

We hosted a memorial service for my father, where family and friends came from everywhere attended and paid tribute. His old coach and fellow athletes shared memories of experiences they had with my father. My nephew flew in from Las Vegas, as did his father, my brother, from Texas.

After the memorial, I was left with my thoughts and many unanswered questions about the brothers and sisters he claimed I had, including the twin boys he spoke about often. Where were they? Despite the many years that have passed, I'm still left with the question of where my siblings are. The question of why he did what he did in not being in their lives is futile because he was not a man of structure. He was disciplined in his craft and in his work, however, he had no sense of family structure as it related to his own tribe.

...

On February 1, 2018, Facebook was full of posts memorializing the life of Dennis Edwards, the lead singer from the Temptations who had just died. Edwards vocals on the iconic hit "Poppa Was a Rolling Stone" were even more poignant that day. I received a call from my cousin asking had I seen the Facebook post made by my brother L announcing two newfound brothers he had discovered thanks to home DNA tests. Confused, I asked what brothers? What DNA? "Just look on your brother's Facebook page; it was posted yesterday," she said. I quickly ended the call and hurried to my brother's page, where I noticed the post featured three photos, side by side. The first photo was of my father from his late twenties which I'd had seen many times before. The second photo was of a young man I had never seen before, dressed in a Navy uniform. The last photo was of a woman who also, I had never seen. Curious and anxious, I began to read the post which in summary he said, "thanks to DNA and my brother for finding me." He went on to say how it was our father's last wish to find his brother. As I continued to read, comments mentioned that there was another brother living in Chicago, which proved to be true.

Filled with emotions, I immediately called my oldest sister Jamie and our other siblings. The group texts and phone calls between family and close friends went on for days. Dozens of people commented on the post, most of whom were congratulating my brother for having connected with his new brother. However, there was one post that celebrated my father as a player who had many women. That person's comment completely trivialized the reality that he had all these children and the pain that he had left them all behind. It's bad enough to be a player and hurt women, but involving children changes the game, and no one's pain should be glorified.

We had been through a lot with my father, and my mother just wanted us to be okay. She wasn't concerned about what folks thought. Of course, there was some shock, because although I was aware that my father had several more children, I hadn't realized how close to where we lived one of those brother's had been. Him having been raised in the same town caught me off guard. Despite the mix of emotions, I was mainly excited that they had found us. Although having it all play out publicly on Facebook wasn't the best way to find out, we had all connected, and would continue communicating by phone, text, and a family chat that one of the brothers set up for us. It was nice way to get to know one another.

I was unable to attend our Smith family reunion in Texas the summer of 2019. My mother was having surgery and I was caring for her during her recovery. My sister Jamie, however, attended the reunion with my aunts, who are actually my father's first cousins, but have always been like aunts to us. My brother from Texas, along with both of our newfound brothers from North Carolina and Chicago were also there.

Both of my brothers are older than me. My brother who lives in Chicago was born in Canada a year before me. He's an activist and businessman who also dabbles in the music in the entertainment industry. He reminds me of my father in the sense that he wears many hats in his professional life and has been successful in doing so. He stays busy fighting injustice, advocating for individual's rights and freedoms, and simply offering words of truth and encouragement to those who need it. My brother from North Carolina was born in between my brother James (my parents only son) and my brother L in Texas (with whom I share a father). He is a retired combat veteran, and a former firefighter. I believe it was his DNA that was matched with the brother in Chicago, and then ultimately to our uncle, my father's brother. I was proud of what I learned about my brothers. Jamie and family had nothing but great things to say about them both. It sounded as if the family had an awesome time, and the brothers enjoyed getting to know their family. We continue to keep in touch, and we are looking forward to a time we can all see each other.

The winter of 2019 revealed another surprise; again, through Facebook we discovered we had another brother who was also born and raised in Stockton, and who still lived there. My brother L's post read: "Imagine playing basketball which'yo patnas, and the guys on the court who you say are your brothers really turn out to be your actual blood brothers." My brother in North Carolina and my brother in Texas often played basketball together when they were youngsters with the kid from Stockton who turned out to be their brother. These three childhood friends didn't know until recently that they are brothers. Two of the friends used to joke that they were twin brothers because they looked alike, but they had no idea that they really were brothers. I believe our brother in Stockton's DNA was matched with the brother in North Carolina and the brother in Chicago.

Jamie and I met up with our newfound brother in Stockton at the bowling alley, on the same day we found out about him. We were all so happy and excited to see each other. We hugged and hugged and talked and took pictures. His mannerisms were those of my father. His sense of humor was that of my father. When he laughed and talked it was like my father. It was like hanging out with my father. We had a good time that night. He had no problem blending right in with the rest of family, and he introduced us to some of his friends and family. He and I keep in touch, as I try to check in on all the brothers from time to time.

It was a lot for all of us to take in and I had so many questions. I had moments of melancholy. Wondering what my brothers' lives were like growing up. Did they have nice parents? Did they feel loved by their families? Did they ever feel as if something was missing? Not that my life was anything close to perfect, but it was better than what it could have been.

I first met my brother from North Carolina the summer of 2020, amid the COVID pandemic, at my mother's home, who welcomed our brothers with open arms. He had rode his Harley across country with his best friend. My husband and I prepared them a good, home cooked meal to go with the good conversation they were enjoying with my mother and my sister Jamie. I was happy to see they appeared to feel right at home. My brother is very tall and intelligent like my dad, with some similar features and plenty of his mannerisms. He was very reserved and respectful but conveyed a great sense of caring and honestly. He shared stories from his childhood and his life overall. His life story is gripping.

My other newfound brother, who lives in Stockton, also stopped by to meet my mother, spend time with his sisters and reunite with his childhood friend who he had recently learned was his blood brother. He is also a kind and caring person. He is elated to have sisters and to provide that protective brotherly love. His wit and intellect were directly inherited from our father.

We talked for hours, asking, and answering questions, most concentrating on my father and his many children. We learned about each of our childhoods and the direction our lives had taken. We listened as the two brothers cracked on each other about the classes they shared in high school. They even attended the same church, and their adopted families knew each other very well.

The day after that beautiful visit, my brother from North Carolina, jumped on his Harley and headed to Las Vegas to meet our brother James (my mother and father's son). Ironically, not only did our brothers share the same name, but each of their best friends shared the same name as well. The brothers met and bonded over a bottle of Jack Daniel's Whiskey, shared stories and enjoyed each other's company.

My father knew he had other kids, but he made no attempt to locate them, or even acknowledge them to us until we were adults. It hurt me to think about that. I witnessed the last twenty years of my father's life, and he was a tortured and broken soul. I believe that much of the torment that he inflicted on himself by drinking, smoking, using drugs and not taking proper care of himself, was born of the guilt and shame that he felt over the long trail of pain, hurt, neglect and tears that he left behind. But regardless of whether he was in our lives for short seasons of never at all, we all persevered.

My pastor who delivered the eulogy at my father's memorial service asked me to describe my father in a few words. I responded that my father was a renaissance man, which is defined as a person with many talents or areas of knowledge. Despite all my father's accomplishments as an artist, athlete, and teacher. He had failed at his most important task - being a father to all of his children. I don't know what my brother's lives may have been had they met their father or been in their lives. I can only bear witness to the impact he had on my mother's children. I still struggle with many unanswered questions about my father.

"The sins of the father are to be laid upon the children."

William Shakespeare

Epilogue

When the smoke had cleared, and the damage was done, we all grew up and were able to move forward with our lives, regardless of the hands we were dealt. We faced many obstacles as most people do and we overcame them.

I am still left wondering how my life might have been different had my father not shot my mother, had my parents been able to make their marriage work and had he been more present in my life as I was growing up. But the adage says that "you can't miss what you never had," and given my father's history, perhaps life played out as it should have. I had all the love and nurturing I could ask for from my mother, my grandmother, my siblings, and our village, and never felt as if I missed or needed my father around anyway. As I've grown and matured, I have come to realize that, in fact, I needed a good father or at least a good father figure. I realized that a lot of the choices that I made during those years I was growing up were a reflection of the lack of discipline, guidance, and watchful eye that I so needed from both a mother and a father. However, I don't allow the negative aspects of my family's past to define who I am today.

I have resolved to remain in touch with my newfound brother's as often as I can. All of mother's children are still very close, and I talk to my mother several times every day. We visit with both sides of our family and cherish the time that we are here with one another. We embrace the traditions and customs of cooking and family socials, all the lessons that Mama and Granny taught us, and what we've learned about ourselves and our family along the way. We will pass along to our children the truths of our existence even when they may seem too painful for us too bear. My family still has a lot of healing to do. Many issues have not been resolved, and secrets and untold truths which will likely never be addressed. My lifelong journey has been full of both triumphs and tragedies but discovering peace and pursuing closure for myself has helped me endure and thrive. I have had to acknowledge my wrongs and accept the things that I couldn’t change or had no control over. But greatest of all, I learned to forgive myself and forgive others. Pray about it and then give it to God.

Acknowledgements

Thank you, Lord, for watching over me, and for all that you have done for me. None of this would be possible without you.

Thanks, and love to:

My mother, Alice, the strongest woman I know. Thank you for what you have taught me. The love and support that you have always given me and the unconditional love that you have never stop showing.

My sisters, Jamie & Jai, who are like my second mothers, thank you for protecting me, taking care of me, and loving my children like your own.

My brother James R. Smith my superhero. Thank you for always taking the time to be a big brother to me when I was a growing up. You've always had my back.

My two beautiful daughters, Saundria and Melo. Thank you for loving me and believing in me.

My husband, Malcolm, who has been with me through so much. I appreciate you, your love and support, thank you for pushing me to finish this book.

My aunts, uncles, cousins, relatives, sisters, brothers, and close friends. Who have been there for me and my family. Thank you. I deeply appreciate you.

My cousin Christopher Bolding. Our relationship has grown over the years to one that I will always cherish. Thank you for all your work and help with editing this book.

My brothers, my heart is filled to know that we have connected and I'm optimistic about our future journey moving forward as a family.

My father James Earl. Thank you for giving me life.

www.ingramcontent.com/pod-product-compliance
Ingram Content Group UK Ltd.
Pitfield, Milton Keynes, MK11 3LW, UK
UKHW022019190726
13853UKWH00005B/2017

9 798985 172409